Acknowledgements

Grateful thanks are due to the following people without whose encouragement, help and support this book would never have been completed.

Bonnie Benson, Mike Koen, Laura, Cheryl, Marge and all the wonderful staff at Quilters' Resource, Chicago, U.S.A.

Carole Binding and Jeremy Froy of Carole Design, Barton-le-Clay, Beds. U.K.

Elizabeth Counsell West of EQS ... European Quilting Supplies, Leicester. U.K.

Kaleidoscope Fabrics International Limited, Hamilton. Scotland.

Reto Linder of Mettler threads, Germany.

Peartree Quilters ... especially Sue Martin for proof reading and assistance in making the Nasturtium, Day lily, Apple Blossom, Daffodil and Pansy quilts.

The fabrics used to complete the quilts are mainly from the fabric ranges of the following companies,

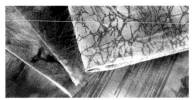

Gold marbled effects by
Hoffman Fabrics, California.

Blended colour 'Aurora' by
R.J.R. Fabrics.

Variable dye plain colours by
Timeless Treasures Ltd.

'Beautiful Blooms' © Angela Madden.
ISBN 0 952 106094
First Edition May 2003.

Distribution in U.S.,
Quilters' Resource Inc.,
2211 N. Elston Ave.
Chicago. Il 60614. U.S.A.
312 278 5795

Published by
M.C.Q. Publications,
Old Barn Cottage, Luton Road, Kimpton,
Herts. SG4 8HA. U.K.

'Earth laughs in flowers'
– Ralph Waldo Emmerson

Angela Madden's
Beautiful
Blooms

'One touch of nature
makes the whole world kin'
– William Shakespeare

Contents

Introduction

'I hope that while so many people are out smelling the flowers, someone is taking time to plant some'
Henry Rappaport.

This appliqué technique requires no special needlework or artistic expertise. Abandoning the convention that requires appliqué edges to be turned under, fusible web and machine stitching are combined to produce classy images and save time.

Before traditionalists throw up their hands in horror visualising stiff, glue laden creations, be assured that quality is not sacrificed. The fusible cannot be detected in the finished article. Quilts made using this method are every bit as soft and friendly as anyone could desire.

Needleworkers today are lucky to have the products of our age. New techniques, tools, machines and inventions enable fabric to be used in ways unimagined by our grandmothers. Quilters from the past would marvel at our possibilities. I do not believe that they would reject them all in favour of 'traditional' ways.

These completed blooms do not take forever to finish, leaving time for you to be a person as mentioned above who 'plants' i.e. sews flowers gracefully accepting compliments from those who, whilst 'smelling,' i.e. admiring, wrongly assume the creative process was both complex and difficult. There are no 'brownie points' in heaven for doing things the hard way.

Read completely through the technique instructions before starting, and you will enjoy the journey as much as the arrival.

If sewing is not successful, classy and fun ...

... why do it?

Requirements

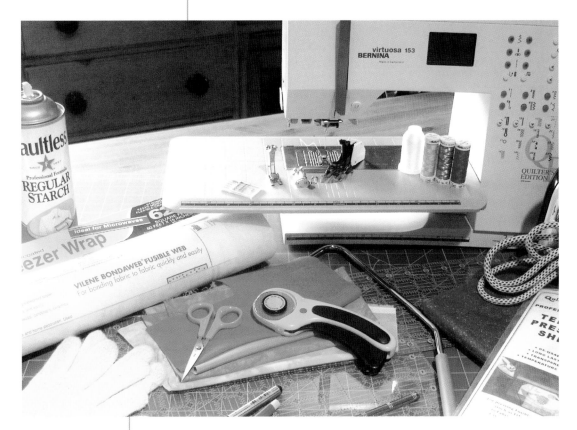

Rotary cutter.

Rotary cutting ruler.

Cutting board.

Quilter's square ruler.

Teflon pressing sheet.

Hard pressing board. *(optional)*

Iron.

Sewing machine.

Sewing machine knee lift. *(optional)*

Black felt pen.

Chalk pencil.

Bondaweb fusible web.

Small sharp scissors.

Nylon monofilament *(invisible)* thread.

Sizes 60/8 and 70/11 machine needles.

Open toe embroidery, quilting and walking machine feet.

Embroidery threads.

Firm cotton fabrics which do not go 'fluffy' at the edges when cut.

Spray starch.

Quilting gloves *(with rubber studs on the fingers)*.

Teaspoon.

Safety pins.

Freezer paper – a waxed paper obtainable from quilt shops or supermarkets in the U.S.

Preparing fusible web

▶ The sparing use of fusible web ensures the success of this technique. It provides a temporary bond, replacing pins in the first stage of assembly. Once all the fabric sections have been fused the second stage can be completed ...

i.e. ... *trouble free* sewing.

Many different fusibles are available today, each with their own characteristics suited to different purposes. Experimentation helps to understand the strengths and limitations of each.

I prefer 'Bondaweb' (also called 'Vliesofix' or 'Wonder Under'), a fusible web attached to backing paper. When ironed to fabric it sticks at most heat settings. The resulting bond is strong enough to hold fabrics in position for stitching but can be broken if required and the fabrics separated.

Folding and handling can part fusible from the backing paper, making it difficult to use. For this technique buy Bondaweb from a roll rather than folded in a packet, wrapping it around a cardboard tube to prevent damage until you are ready to use it.

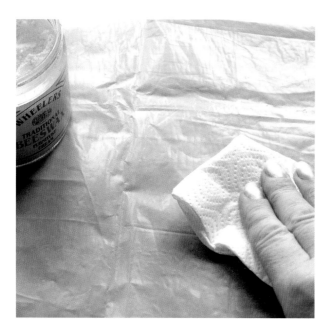

◀ If the adhesion of fusible to paper can be increased, the separation problem is decreased. Future handling is then trouble free, and 'stickability' is unaffected.

A teflon coated pressing sheet, available from quilt shops or supermarkets, where they are sold as non-stick cookery aids, makes this possible.

Each time the sheet is used a quick, light spray or application of wax polish on a paper towel will make it even more non-stick.

◀ Lay a piece of Bondaweb *paper side uppermost* on the pressing sheet.

The setting of the iron is vital to success:

– too cool and nothing will happen,

– too hot and the fusible sticks to the sheet.

Begin by setting the iron to 'cool,' then gradually increase the heat by small increments as necessary. Watch for signs of the paper darkening and becoming transparent indicating that the fusible is beginning to melt. The temperature at which this starts to happen is ideal.

Lightly iron the fusible to the teflon sheet so that the colour change is visible throughout.

▶ If the heat was appropriate the fusible and teflon sheet will separate easily.

Look at the fusible and compare it to a piece which has not been heated.

New Bondaweb fusible looks dull. When heated as described, it becomes noticibly shiny. This makes fusible and paper easy to tell apart, decreasing the chance of accidentally getting it stuck to the iron.

Shiny fusible is better adhered to the paper.

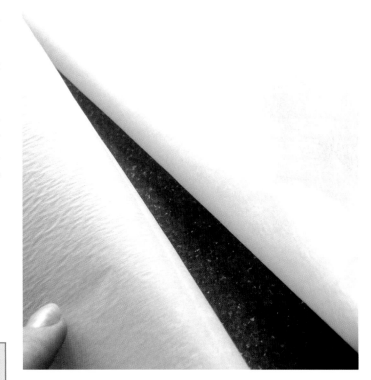

However ...

If the iron was hotter than 'just right'....

plan B overleaf will be useful.

▶ If fusible and sheet are difficult to separate, the iron was too hot.

Never try to pull them apart. This will only tear and damage the Bondaweb,

... instead try 'Plan B'

Roll fusible and sheet as one and place in a freezer for a few minutes.

This rapidly cools and hardens the fusible.

◀ Take them from the freezer and try to separate them again. Hopefully they will just fall apart. The fusible will be shiny as before.

If they still will not separate do not resort to force,
... try 'plan C'.

With paper on top, lay them again on the ironing board. Using something blunt, such as the handle of a rotary cutter or scissors, gently rub over the paper. This pressure should separate the layers without causing damage.

The paper will lighten in colour where it has separated.

If that still does not work the iron must have been red hot. Pull the fusible away and dispose of it. Clean the sheet with a paper towel and try again. This time use a much lower heat setting.

Heat treating all Bondaweb in this way when it is first bought will make it robust and a pleasure to use.

Preparing designs

◀ Designs are provided at page size, but the bigger the design the easier it is to handle, the faster it is to complete and the more satisfying it is as a first project.

Big designs create maximum impact.

The speediest most efficient enlargement methods are computer scanning or photocopying. Specialist photocopying shops can enlarge to the size of architect's plans at one go.

Alternatively, a pattern copy can be cut into many equal sections and individually enlarged before taping back together. Enlargement guides are printed on each pattern.

▶ The enlarged design is the master plan for the project and remains intact throughout.

From your master plan trace the design on the dull side of freezer paper using a black pen for clarity.

(The easy way to join freezer paper pieces together to increase the sheet size, is by ironing over-lapping edges)

Visibility will be clearer against a window or by using a light box. This tracing will be cut up providing all the templates.

When making the tracing include all the pattern markings.

▶Registration marks are present on all internal lines in a design. It is important to include them all as they will help to match joins correctly.

There are no registration marks around the outline of patterns as these lines will not be matched to anything.

Should a pattern piece get lost during assembly simply retrace the missing section. Registration marks will ensure that the replacement piece will still be an exact fit.

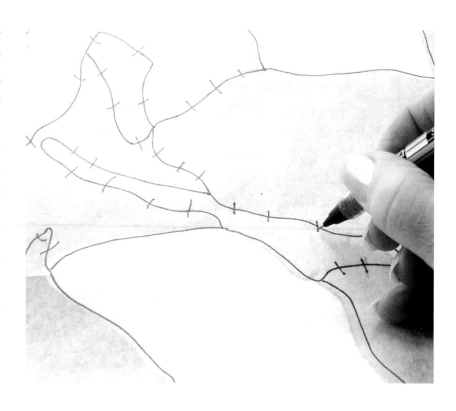

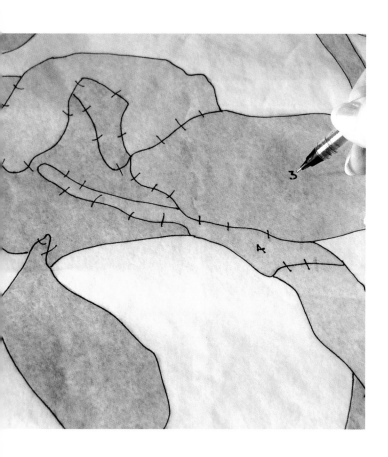

◀ Pattern pieces are numbered for easy identification. Patterns with fewer pieces and smooth outlines are the fastest and easiest to complete. You could consider taking a short cut of tracing several pieces as one, ignoring dividing lines. This speeds the completion time but reduces colour variety. Missed lines could be replaced later as quilting lines.

Pattern colours are only provided as a guide. Alternative choices can produce original variations.

Colour suggestions in patterns are pale to ensure that all markings will show through for photocopying.

You may choose to write the colour on each pattern piece. (Circled numbers indicate colour in this photo sequence.)

Cutting Templates

◄ There is no special order to follow in completing a design.

Cutting can begin anywhere.

Cut accurately, as these pattern pieces are templates and will control the final result.

▶ The shiny side of freezer paper is ironed to the right side of the fabric. The paper always lies on top of the work showing the registration marks which help to match joins.

There is an ideal temperature for ironing freezer paper to fabric:

– too cool and it will not stick for long,

– too hot and it is difficult to remove.

Experiment so that you will become familiar with this, as it is necessary for the paper to remain stuck to the fabric until all joins are fused ready for stitching.

Most freezer paper can be stuck and removed several times before the power to stick is lost. This enables templates to be re-used several times.

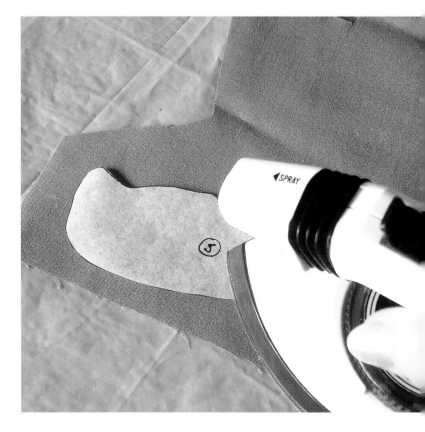

Adding seam allowances

▶ Choose a working method. Either ... two neighbouring pieces can be cut from the tracing, stuck to fabric and joined. Further pieces are then cut individually and added. This method is ideal where time or space is limited. Fused sections can be pinned to the master pattern for safe keeping.

Or ... single or multiple patterns can be entirely cut up at the start. For multiples, stack additional freezer paper sheets behind and pinned to the traced copy. Place a pin in each individual pattern section to keep pieces together.

Cut through all layers, laying each batch of pieces correctly on the master pattern.

◀ Numbering cloned pieces and ironing them to the same fabric in batches saves time. Registration marks are lost on the additional copies. Joining the traced copy first and repeating the move through all the clones enables the traced copy to be a guide. If there is a problem, trace the registration lines on extra pieces as required.

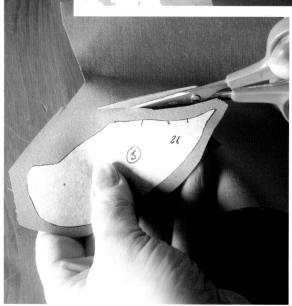

◀ Freezer paper stabilises fabric. Grain direction does not have an effect. Templates can be positioned to suit colour choice, pattern or economy of fabric. However, should you wish to match all grain lines, mark guide lines on the tracing before beginning to cut.

A fabric seam allowance must be added as you cut around each template.

The traditional quilter's ¼ in. is excessive, but ⅛ in. is too small. Somewhere between is just right. Make a sample to help clarify the best size to ensure strength when bonded without adding bulk and stiffness.

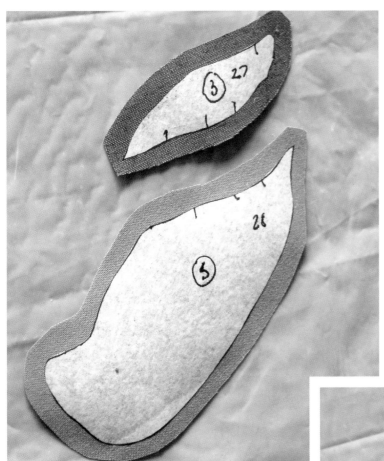

◄ The edge to be joined is easily identified when neighbouring shapes are positioned alongside each other.

At every join one piece overlaps the other bringing the paper edges together. The registration marks connect, indicating a perfect match.

Colour is important. A good rule to bear in mind is 'dark on top of light'. This prevents a dark colour showing through a light top layer.

(However, it is not always possible to follow this rule, or prevent some light fabrics showing through another light top layer).

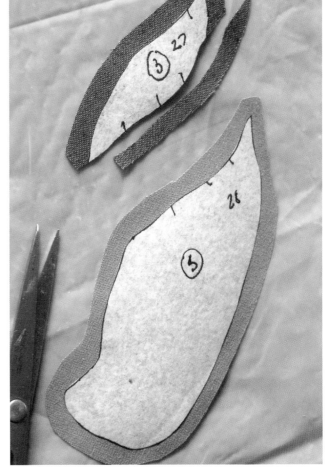

▶ The seam allowance is cut away from the piece which will lie on top along the edge to be joined.

Always check exactly where a cut begins and ends. All joins are not as straightforward as this example. Mark the paper to guide you.

Cutting fusible strips

◀ Cut strips of Bondaweb about a scant ¼ in. wide from the piece which has been heat treated.

These do not need to be perfectly straight.

Only cut sufficient for current needs as Bondaweb is easier to store in one piece than in little strips.

▶ Place the section from which the seam allowance has been cut wrong side up on the teflon sheet. Iron a strip of fusible along the edge with no allowance. It will not matter if the fusible pleats or buckles as you follow contours. If one piece of fusible is too short add another.

It is important to have the fusible extend beyond the fabric edge as it will bind fibres together and prevent loose threads poking out.

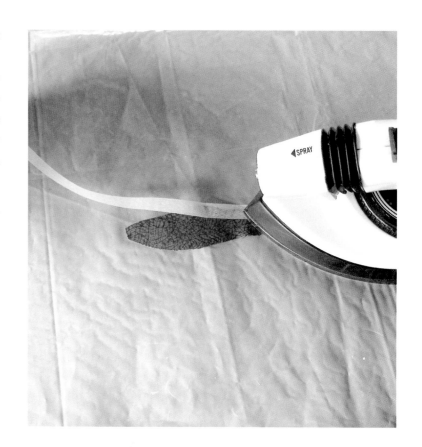

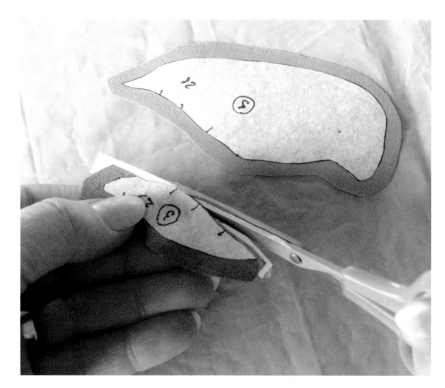

▶Trim away the excess fusible which juts beyond the paper's edge.

Ensure that no fabric extends beyond the paper either, so that the join will be tight and exact.

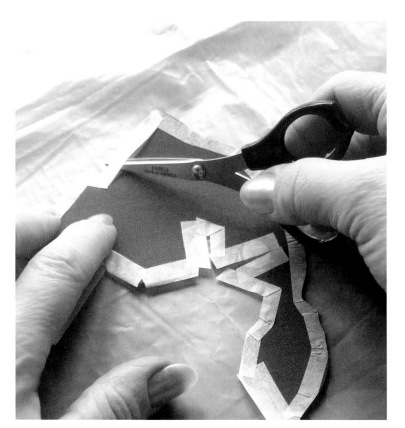

◀ The paper backing can now be removed from the fusible strip.

Sliding the blade of a scissors under the paper can be the easiest way of lifting the paper.

Quickly dispose of these used bits of paper. It is difficult to distinguish them from unused fusible strips, and they can become a nuisance.

Joining pieces together

▶ Unite the pieces, matching the registration lines at the join. Iron to bond the seam. Always use the teflon sheet when doing this.

Repeat the technique with neighbouring pattern pieces until the flower is completed.

Assembly is easier if small pieces are joined first to make a bigger section. The bigger sections can them be joined to complete the whole.

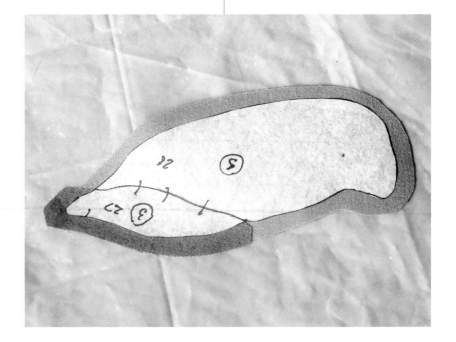

◀ The last stage of assembly is the application of fusible strips around the outside edge of the flower to prepare it for bonding to its background.

On larger designs it is more convenient to trim and fuse the exposed edges as you go along, rather than waiting until the design is completed. As long as edges are all fused, the order of work is not important.

The finished design will be strong enough to handle as an item. It can be safely rolled inside the master pattern until ready for use.

Choosing backgrounds

◀ Any design will look good if used alone, but many unique combinations can also be made up by using several flower designs together.

▶ A fused flower is portable making it possible to experiment placing it against different coloured backgrounds.

Make sure all parts of the design can be clearly seen. This helps those who do not feel confident working with colour.

The flower can even be taken to your favourite fabric shop and tried against different fabrics before purchase, providing a golden opportunity to canvass the opinion of others.

Flower motifs can be appliquéd to clothing, bags, furnishings, and traditionally pieced quilt tops.

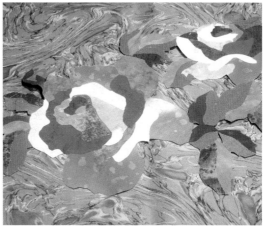

Drafting an oval

▶ Ovals make great frames for flowers but are often considered difficult to draft accurately. This easy method requires no special equipment. Try it first on a sheet of scrap paper.

Decide the measurement, top to bottom and side to side, of an oval which will fit on the scrap paper.

A pleasing oval is one which is neither too skinny nor too fat.

Draw a north/south line equalling the length of the oval.

(a measurement which divides easily in half is a good choice.)

Label this line AB.

Mark the centre.

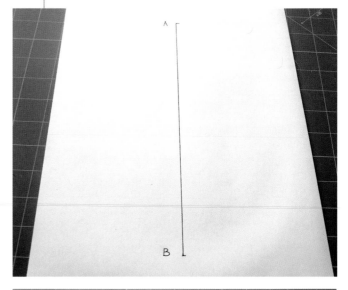

▶ Draw an east/west line equalling the width of the oval.

Match the centre of this line to the centre of AB.

Label this new line XY.

Mark the centre crossing point C.

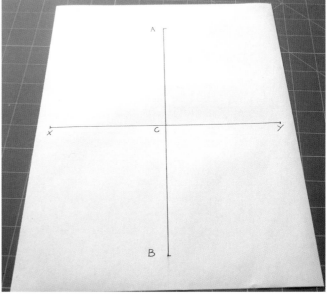

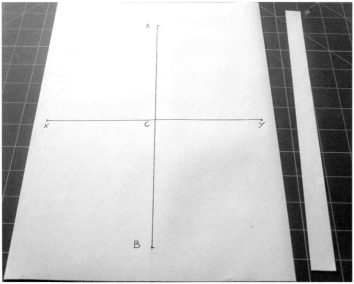

◀ Cut a 'ruler' from scrap paper which is a few inches longer than AC and has straight sides.

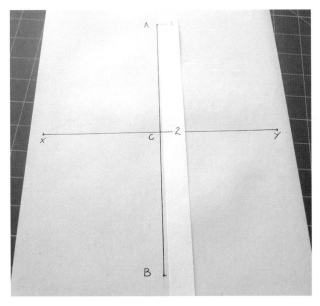

Lay the paper 'ruler' alongside line AB.

Accurately mark the position of A as 1, and C as 2 on the ruler.

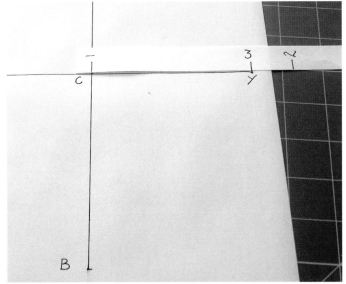

Lay the ruler beside line XY placing point 1 at C.

Mark the position of Y as 3 on the ruler.

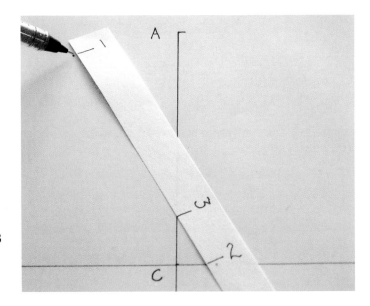

Position the ruler as shown with point 3 touching AC and point 2 touching CY.

Draw a dot at point 1.

▶ Slide the ruler so that 3 moves further down AC whilst 2 still touches line CY.

This will alter the position of 1.

Mark another dot at this new position.

Repeat as necessary, creating an arc of dots forming one quarter of the oval.

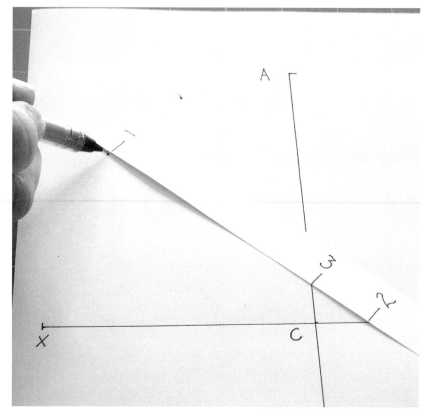

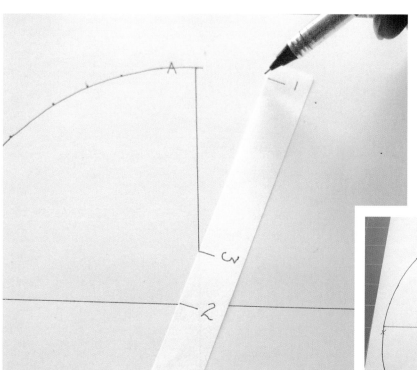

◀ Rotate the ruler placing it in each quarter in turn and drawing more dots.

Linking all the dots will complete the oval at the chosen size.

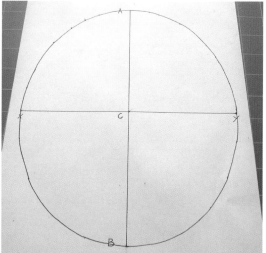

Large fabric ovals

The same principle can be adapted to draft ovals suitable for larger projects.

Measure the length and width of the flower design you plan to use.

Add extra to AB and XY to allow space around the design. Extra space at the top and bottom of the flower will increase the oval shape.

▶ Take a piece of freezer paper large enough to accommodate the proposed oval.

Fold it in half, then in half again, flattening the folds creating north/south and east/west lines. The middle is now obvious where the folds cross.

▶ Measure and draw lines AB and XY on the folds.

Mark C in the centre where they cross.

▶ Once again cut a paper ruler and use it to mark the position of the arc of dots in one quarter.

Join the dots to form a quarter oval.

Stop drawing dots at this point as it is not necessary to mark the other three quarters.

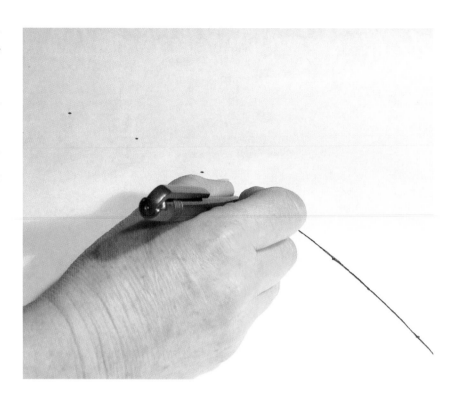

◀ Re-fold the paper into four along the same folds, making sure that the marked quarter oval line is visible on the outside.

Place pins at intervals to prevent the paper from moving.

Cut along the quarter oval line through all the layers of paper.

Iron the paper oval to fabric.

Cut exactly around the oval. It is not necessary to add a seam allowance.

▶ Position the completed flower centrally in the fabric oval.

Iron to fuse ready for stitching.

Iron strips of Bondaweb to the edge of the fabric oval on the wrong side.

Trim excess fusible and remove the backing paper.

◀ Fold the fabric oval and background fabric into quarters and finger press north/south and east/west folds.

Pin the wrong side of the oval to the right side of the background fabric matching the folds.

Finally iron the edge of the oval to fuse it in position ready for stitching.

Positioning flowers

▲ Freezer paper ovals and other shapes can be useful aids when positioning groups of flowers.

Here rose motifs have been arranged around an oval to create a frame. The freezer paper was ironed to the background fabric and roses were arranged a uniform distance from each other.

The same parts of each flower touched the oval.

When all motifs were correctly placed they were fused. The paper oval was then removed and could be re-used.

▼ Circles can be drafted by the same method if AB and XY are the same length.

A freezer paper circle can also be used to help position flower motifs.

In these examples both fabric and paper were folded into quarters and the folds used as positioning guides.

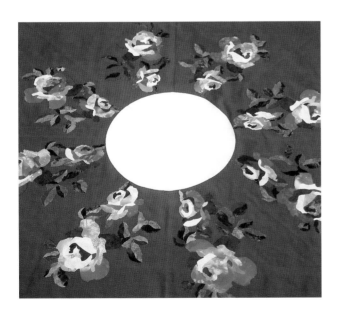

Sewing seams

▶Sewing flowers is easy using a tiny zig zag stitch. Visibility is ensured by using an open toe embroidery foot.

Nylon monofilament thread disguises stitches, and blends with all colours.

A neutral colour thread fills the bobbin and the machine tension is set so the bobbin thread is not visible on the right side of the work.

A fine needle *(size 60/8 makes small holes.)* This is not a general purpose needle and can break easily if stressed, but is ideal for this specialist job. Larger needles sew well but make bigger, more noticible holes.

Once again a 'knee lift' makes rounding curves and corners swift and efficient.

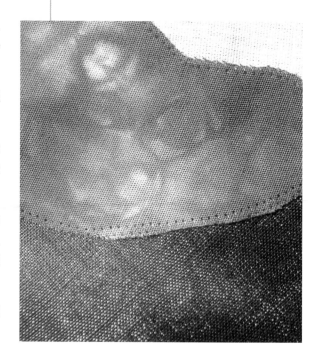

◀ The perfect stitch seals the edge of the fabric shape, is difficult to see, and is strong enough to hold the fabrics together permanently.

A 1.5 stitch width and 1.0 stitch length is about right. Sew a test sample using the project fabrics. Judge by appearance and not by numbers, as all machine settings do not produce the same results. Use bigger or smaller stitches if it looks better.

The needle should enter just beyond the outside edge of the top fabric then swing in a short distance encasing the cut edge. Constantly check that you are sewing on the top fabric. If the stitching falls only on the lower fabric the join will not be secure.

Sometimes light can play tricks. If in doubt rub a scissors or fingernail against the fabric edge to make sure.

Avoid piercing the fabric edge during stitching.

This makes threads stick out and spoils clean-cut shapes. If loose threads are unsightly trim them close to the stitching with sharp scissors. Be careful not to cut the thread.

◀ Before starting to stitch, hold the work up to the light to check that all the seams are robust. If there is too little seam allowance or even a gap it will show. This is the time to remedy the problem and no one will ever suspect. Fuse a small piece of matching fabric over the back of any problem join.

This patch needs to be big enough to cover the join with a bit to spare either side, but not so big that it causes a stiff patch which could be visible from the right side.

For strength it will be necessary to stitch on both the top and lower fabric through the patch. A safety pin placed at the spot will help to remind you to do this.

▶ Zig zag around the shape over the patch on the top fabric.

Return and stitch again this time on the lower fabric. The double stitching will anchor the fused patch to both fabrics creating a strong join. It will not be detectable once the quilting has been completed.

◀ Stitch around the largest shapes in the design first, e.g. this might be a whole flower head or large leaf. This will enable the fabric behind it to be cut away from the wrong side about ¼in. inside the stitching.

A single layer of fabric always feels softer and 'puffs' out better when quilted.

Many shapes in the design (e.g. *stalks*) are too small or narrow to consider cutting away the fabric behind.

Cut wherever it is sensible and ignore the remainder.

▶ Sew three or four very small straight stitches before starting to zig zag securing the thread and preventing it from coming undone.

To end off revert to straight stitch with the needle positioned on the outside of the shape and complete three or four very close stitches to fasten off.

The threads can be trimmed close to the fabric on both sides.

▶ Once the outside of a flower has been stitched and the back fabric cut away, the seams inside that flower can be zig zagged.

(if they were sewn first the fabric behind could not be removed.)

Be careful that you do not skip any seams when stitching. Short ones are especially easy to miss.

Additional lighting at the machine will clarify where you have stitched and where you have not. Checking the back of the work also shows up omissions.

A missed seam is not a total disaster.

Un-stitched seams look different and can be identified at the quilting stage. Sewing the offending seam using zig zag as the quilting stitch will invisibly solve the problem.

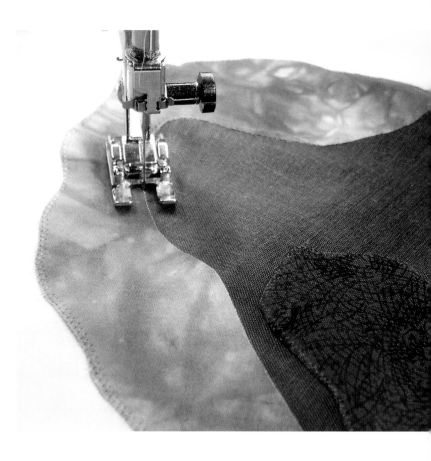

◀ Rolling the edge of the quilt top upwards over itself in a circle around the work ... *(looking rather like a 'pizza crust')* makes turning to stitch in different directions much easier. It also prevents edges straying under the work and getting sewn as double layers.

Wavy borders

▶ Borders enhance a quilt as frames enhance paintings. Straight borders can be sewn on as strips, but a more unusual wavy edged border is possible using this technique.

Decide on the finished width of the proposed wavy border adding ½ in. to provide for seam allowances on both sides.

Rotary cut four border strips at this width. The length will depend upon the style of corner planned.

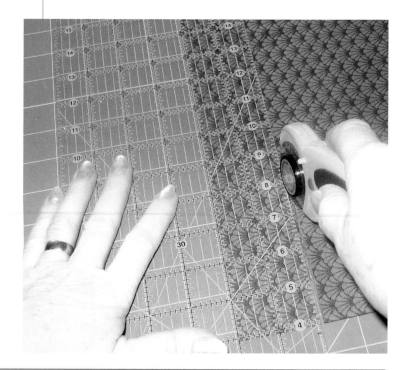

Mitred corners require four border lengths cut to match the quilt sides plus double the border width. Therefore a wall hanging measuring 36in. wide by 42in. long with a 3in. border would require,

> 2 strips of   36 + 3+3 = 42in. for the width and ...

> 2 strips of   42 + 3+3 = 52in. for the length.

'Log cabin' style corners require

> 2 strips as above for the width and ...

> 2 strips at 42in. for the length with no border allowance added.

◀ Rotary cut sufficient 1in. wide strips of Bondaweb to correspond to the border lengths.

◀ Iron the fusible strips to the wrong side of each border length aligning the edges. When one fusible strip ends add another, butting it up against the first.

Iron on the teflon sheet in case any fusible overlaps the edge.

▶ Lay the fused border strip on the cutting board wrong side up.

Freehand cut a wavy line through the centre of the fusible. The paper will keep the fabric flat and stiff showing exactly where to cut. Draw waves on the backing paper as a guide if you are nervous of spacing them evenly.

Avoid cutting too close to either edge of the fusible. The smooth curve of the wave would be lost if you cut off one edge, and a continuous strip of fusible is needed to create a strong seam join on the other.

Do not throw away the fused wavy strips cut from the outside on the wave they will be useful later.

Attaching borders

▶ Fold the quilt top in four to make sure that the sides match in length. If necessary trim to correct any discrepancy.

Ensure that all four quilt sides are rotary cut absolutely straight, and check that all corners are right angles.

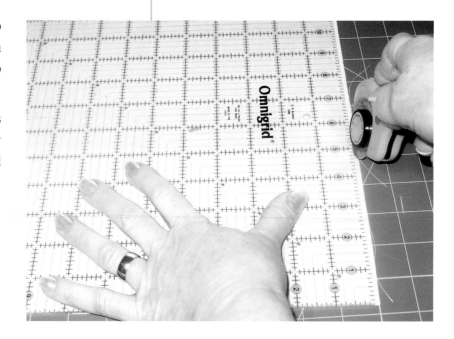

◀ Mark a chalk line 1in. from the edge of the quilt on all sides, on the front of the fabric.

Chalk additional, marks on this line 3in. from all corners in both directions.

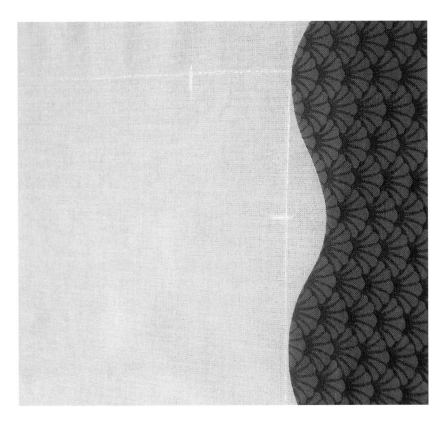

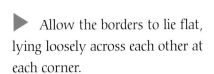 Remove the paper backing from the fusible.

Line up the top of the waves with the chalk line. Iron to bond in place. Fuse all sides up to but not beyond, the 3in. chalk marks.

The corners are left loose to allow them to be mitred.

Should re-alignment ever be necessary, wavy borders can be removed after fusing by softening the fusible with a jet of steam from the iron.

Allow the borders to lie flat, lying loosely across each other at each corner.

Overlap the borders placing the width strip on top of the length strip.

Borders can be fused and stitched in this position creating a 'log cabin' style corner.

Wavy mitres

▶ A novel way to complete the corner is by creating a wavy mitre.

Chalk a wavy line from the inside to the outside corner.

End the line exactly where the two borders cross.

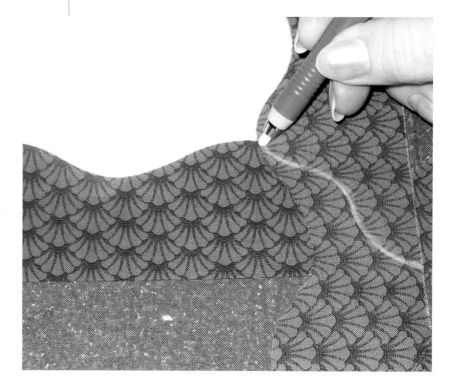

◀ Scissor cut along this chalk line removing the excess fabric from the top border. Fuse Bondaweb to wrong side of the scissor cut.

Iron the wavy mitre, bonding it ready for stitching

A wavy mitre is zig zagged at the same time as the border is attached to the quilt.

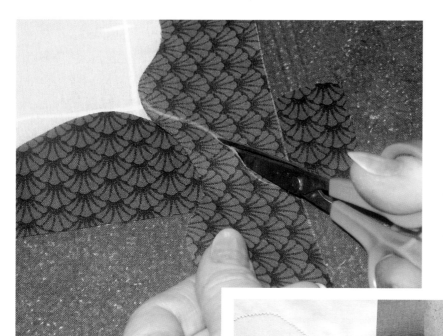

◀ Turn the work to the wrong side after stitching and cut away the excess fabric from the border which lies underneath.

The wavy mitre is now complete.

◀ A straight mitre can also be created by marking a straight line across the corner instead of a wavy one.

▶ Whichever style you decide to use the last job that is required is to trim and square the corner. Using a quilter's square is the surest way to do this.

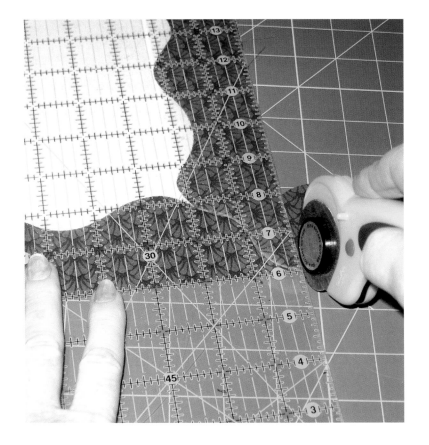

'Slivers'

◀ Offcuts left after cutting wavy borders can be used to create 'slivers' of colour in the backgrounds of quilts.

As the fusible is already applied, they are quick and easy to position ready for stitching.

They can be used as they are or re-cut to a more irregular shape by freehand cutting along the straight side.

◀ Lay 'slivers' wherever you fancy on the background fabric around the flower.

Iron them in place ready for stitching.

▶ 'Slivers' are a quick and easy way to add unexpected flashes of colour in backgrounds.

(Being a person who hates anything to go to waste using them up makes me feel virtuous as well as creative!)

'Wiggly' edging

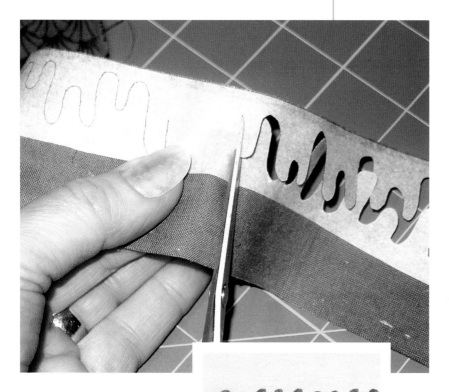

◀ A variation of the wavy edge is the 'wiggly' edge.

The fabric strip is prepared as for waves with a 1in strip of Bondaweb fused along its length.

The wiggles can be cut freehand or following a drawn line. Cuts form a variable series of 's' bends. They are easy to cut with sharp scissors if the fabric is rotated around stationary scissor blades as the direction of the cut changes.

▶ Wiggles create effective contrasting borders.

◀ Once again ready fused offcuts can be used as decoration.

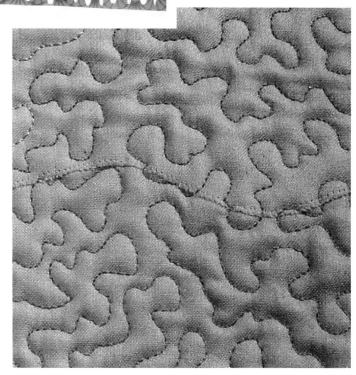

▶ Waves and wiggles are unusual methods of joining fabric to make backgrounds.

Light hits the cut edge in different ways along a wave, making a join between matching fabrics less noticible than a conventional seam. Joins blend into the fabric and are almost invisible especially if they run beneath close quilting.

Wiggles take longer to sew than waves.

▶ The appliqué top is completed and ready to be quilted.

Quilting adds texture bringing the top to life. It is an opportunity to be creative, and original enhancing the design.

Iron the top and backing fabric giving them a liberal spray with starch.

Some quilters stack the three layers, *(backing, batting/wadding and quilt top)* on a table smoothing them flat, and weighting or bulldog clipping the edges to hold them taut during pinning.

◀ I like to lay them on the floor, pinning them into the carpet to ensure that the layers are flat and kept taut.

This guarantees that no surprise wrinkles will develop once the quilting has begun.

This method is hard on the knees but is pretty foolproof.

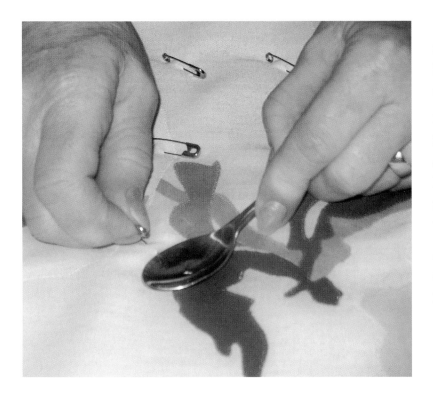

◀ Safety pins offer the fastest and most convenient way to anchor layers together preventing slippage during quilting.

Place a pin through all layers every 2 to 3in. across the quilt. A teaspoon can help to prevent sore fingers on larger items by catching and fastening each pin as it comes up through the fabric.

Safety pins are removed individually during quilting. By the time the top is quilted the pins are all out.

▶ Machine quilting is not difficult to master with a little practice.

Sitting at a comfortable height and having really good lighting also make a difference.

An angled lamp in addition to the machine light is essential for me, by day as well as by night.

Rolling the quilt to fit under the free arm of the machine enables stitching to be completed in the centre.

Bigger quilts may need to be removed and re-rolled several times to complete different parts.

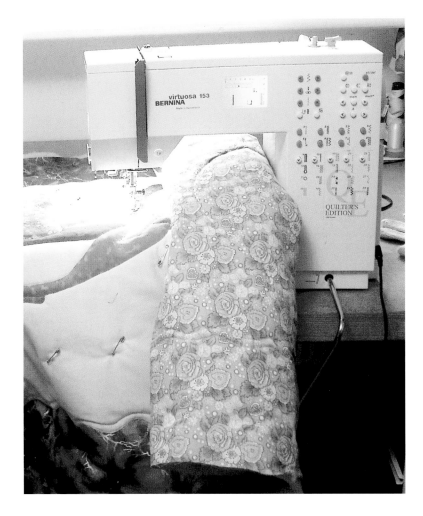

▶ An ironing board beside and at the same height as the sewing table can support the weight of a quilt when sewing large projects.

This prevents the work dragging away from the machine and enables you to have a break and leave without disturbing the work.

One question guides the choice of quilting thread. Is it intended to show up against the fabric on which it lies, or not?

◀ The most invisible thread is nylon monofilament. The next is a perfectly colour matched thread. The most visible is a strongly contrasting colour or one of the beautiful multi-coloured threads.

Be adventurous. Try unusual ones. Sewn threads can look very different from what you expect.

Always use a good branded thread to avoid problems. (*Superior, YLI and Mettler all give great results*). Interesting novelty threads can greatly enhance quilting patterns.

Experiment Experiment, Experiment!

Metallics (*which need to be sewn with a Metallica large eyed needle*) and high sheen threads catch the light.

Thicker decorative threads (*such as YLI 'Candlelight'*) are designed to fill the bobbin and be stitched from the wrong side of the work.

Machine embroidery can also double as quilting adding details too fine for appliqué.

Free quilting

◄ Quilting can be more fun if it is done as 'free' machining using a quilting or darning foot with the feed dogs disengaged.

With the machine no longer confined to sewing in a straight line stitching can be completed without the need for the quilt to be constantly turned.

Stitch length is controlled by the sewer and is a balance between the speed of the machine and the speed at which the fabric is guided.

A few tiny stitches at the start and finish of stitching anchor the thread, preparing it for clipping close to the fabric.

► Quilt with the feed dogs engaged if using a walking foot *(for wrinkle free straight lines and broad curves)* or an open toe embroidery foot *(for maximum visibility)*.

Once again the use of a knee lift speeds the necessary repositioning of the machine foot during changes of direction.

Contour quilting

▶ Quilting adds definition to each shape if stitched 'in the ditch' around the outside of the top fabric.

It pulls the zig zagged edge into the dip, covers any 'whiskers' which may exist and sharpens the appearance.

Begin and end each quilting line with a few minute stitches to secure the thread.

◀ Contour quilting using a parallel line around the perimeter of the design adds importance to the shape and makes it stand out. The appliqué is then clearly separated from any quilting pattern which may surround it.

It is hard to 'over-quilt' a project and very easy to 'under-quilt' one. Leaving large loose areas creates a duvet effect.

Feel challenged to find ways of dividing up dull, blank areas of background into different quilted shapes. Add interest with leaves, clouds, or abstract patterns filled with different quilting textures and thread colours.

Contour quilt beside borders to define the boundaries they create.

Adding texture

▶ One of the most effective ways to add texture to a background is to free stitch a filler pattern. This could be a continuous wavy line or many stop/start patterns such as individual spirals.

The actual pattern might not consist of exact repeats but it should look even throughout the area it fills.

Doodle patterns on scrap paper for ideas.

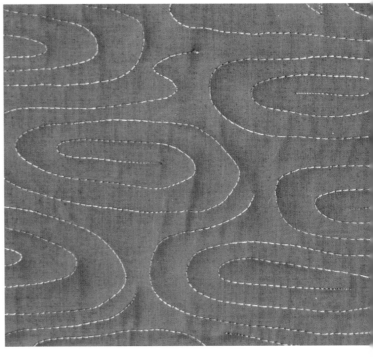

◀ Quilter's gloves with small rubber buttons on the fingers and palms grip the fabric making pattern regularity easier to achieve.

Binding the quilt

◄ The simplest way to bind a quilt is with a continuous length of folded fabric. This creates a double layer binding. Double sided mitres are folded and stitched at each corner as the binding is applied.

Measure the quilt to establish the length of fabric to cut. Most likely shorter lengths will have to be joined.

Rotary cut sufficient strips of fabric at 2½in. wide.

► Diagonal seams will be used to join strips. They are less noticible and less bulky than straight seams.

This will require 45° angles to be cut at both ends of each strip prior to joining. Use the 45° line on the ruler or the cutting board for accuracy.

Ensure that all the angles slant in the same direction when fabric strips are right side up.

▶ Position and join all the strips right sides together as shown.

Cut off the protruding triangle at each end of the seam.

◀ Fold the binding strip in half lengthwise with the seam allowances from joins on the inside.

Spray starch and press the fold flat.

Adding a hanging sleeve

▶ If quilts are to be hung up they will require a 'sleeve' or channel through which a baton can be inserted. Sewn to the quilt back this will help to keep the top rigid and help it to hang straight. The sleeve can be made at this stage and stitched to the quilt as the binding is applied. Using the same backing fabric to make the sleeve will hide it.

Cut a strip 9in. wide for the sleeve.

Calculate the length 1in. shorter than the width of the quilt.

Fold the strip in half lengthwise, wrong side out. Stitch both unfolded ends. Turn fabric to the right side.

Spray starch, press the ends and the fold.

◀ Align the long raw edges of the sleeve with the top edge of the quilt.

Pin both together.

They will be stitched together as the binding is applied.

▶ After the binding has been sewn fold and pin the sleeve so that the fold lies along the quilt top. This will allow a little slack to accommodate the hanging baton. The lower edge of the sleeve can then be hand stitched in place.

◀ Working on the back of the quilt align the start of the binding with the middle of the bottom edge.

Straight stitch the binding to the quilt leaving 6in. of binding loose before stitching begins.

The open toe foot will provide maximum visibility. Using the side of the foot as a guide stitch a uniform distance from the edge.

Continue until nearing the first corner. Mark a chalk dot on the sewing line ¼ in. before the end. Stop stitching on the dot.

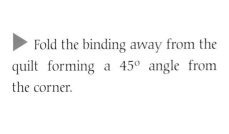 Fold the binding away from the quilt forming a 45° angle from the corner.

▶ Bring the binding back on top of itself creating a new straight fold exactly on top of the edge of the quilt.

The bulk of the binding is now aligned with the next quilt side to be stitched.

The corner 45° fold can be felt underneath the binding. Mark another chalk dot on this fold ¼ in. from the edge

Start stitching along the next quilt side from this dot.

Repeat folds and dots at all remaining corners.

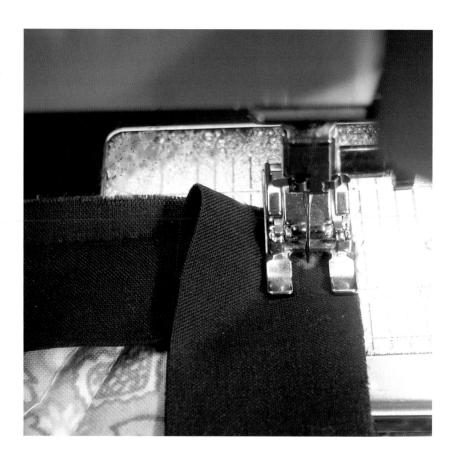

◀ After rounding the final corner continue to approx. 12in. from where the binding stitching begins.

◀ Lay both ends of the binding flat alongside each other.

Allowing for a three to four inch overlap cut the surplus from the straight cut end of the binding.

▶ Overlap the binding ends along the quilt edge ensuring the one with the 45° angled cut is on the top.

Chalk a line on the lower binding alongside this cut.

▶ Open the fold in the lower binding and lay the fabric flat.

Chalk another line parallel to the first and ½in. nearer to the straight cut end of the binding. Carry this line completely across the unfolded fabric.

◀ Cut across the binding on this line.

◀ Fold the quilt right side out, mid way between the two loose ends of the binding.

Match these ends on top of each other at right angles to the quilt.

Pin the quilt in this position.

▶ Position the angled cuts for joining with right sides together. Make sure that the binding has not been twisted.

Stitch the seam and cut off both corner triangles.

Press seam allowances open.

Re-fold the central fold in the binding and press it flat.

▶ Remove the pins from the quilt laying it flat.

The unstitched binding now lies in place along the quilt edge and is exactly the right length to allow stitching to be completed.

The binding is finished off from the front where the stitching will be most visible.

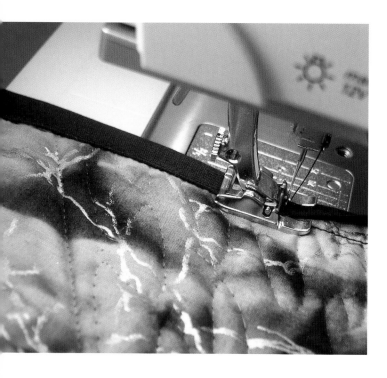

◀ Each quilt side will be sewn in turn starting at the top right hand corner. Fold the top binding to the front immediately before the corner.

Line up the folded edge with the stitching which has just been completed positioning a pin to hold it into the corner.

Bring the binding to the front on the right hand quilt side which is about to be stitched. A mitre will naturally fold at the corner. Check that it is nicely positioned and pin if necessary.

Sew the binding from the mitre, Match the fold with the previous stitching line. Stitch close to the fold.

(If correctly aligned the stitching will appear in the matching position on the back binding).

Continue to the next corner stopping when you reach the stitching which crosses your path.

Repeat on remaining sides.

Blocking the quilt

◀ Blocking is the finishing stage for a quilt. It straightens and smoothes the piece showing the workmanship at its best. It should not be regarded as an optional extra but rather as an essential stage without which no quilt is truly completed.

Blocking has rescued many a doubtful piece of work and has made good quilts look amazing.

When the quilt is finished I lay it on the floor, pinning it straight down into the carpet. If it is pinned just inside the inner edge of the binding it will not be left with holes. It is essential to apply tension, stretching and squaring all sides in turn as they are pinned. Any surface irregularities will be straightened out.

Sides need to be measured and pinned at the correct length.

▶ Turn the iron to a full steam setting and pass it over the quilt holding it a few inches above the surface. *The iron never touches the fabric* but steams it thoroughly through all the layers.

I follow this with a liberal application of spray starch pointing the nozzle upwards, away from the quilt so that no area is directly saturated. This sets all the fibres in place but does not make the quilt stiff.

After leaving the quilt to dry remove the pins and admire your handiwork.

It looks great!

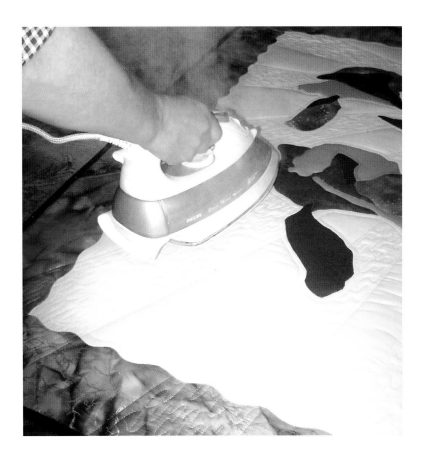

pattern templates

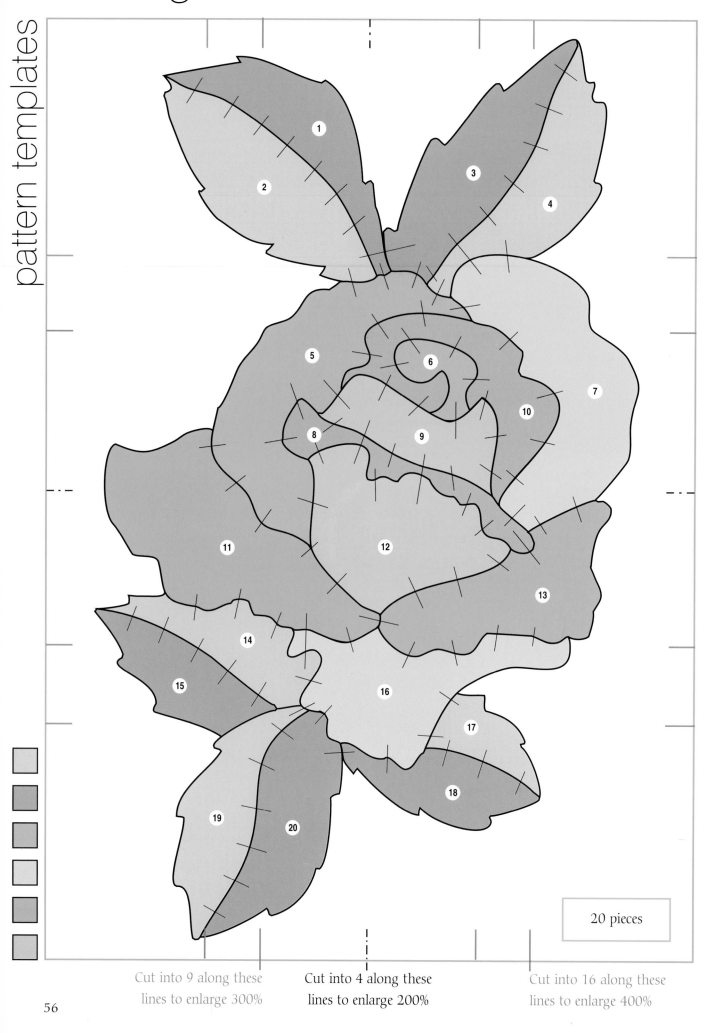

20 pieces

Cut into 9 along these
lines to enlarge 300%

Cut into 4 along these
lines to enlarge 200%

Cut into 16 along these
lines to enlarge 400%

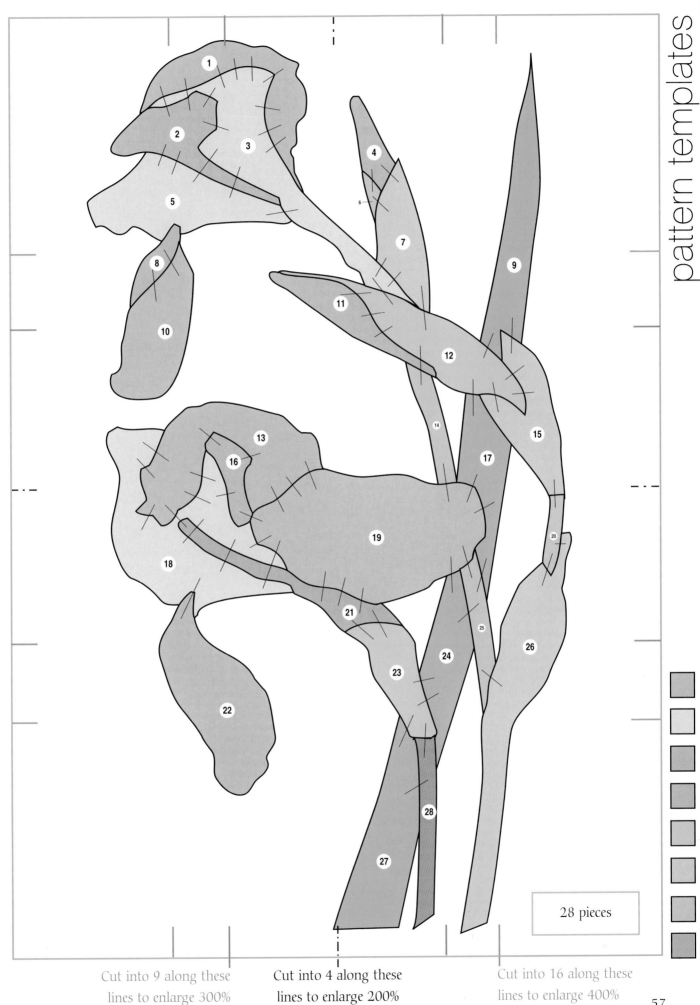

28 pieces

Cut into 9 along these
lines to enlarge 300%

Cut into 4 along these
lines to enlarge 200%

Cut into 16 along these
lines to enlarge 400%

57

Daffodils

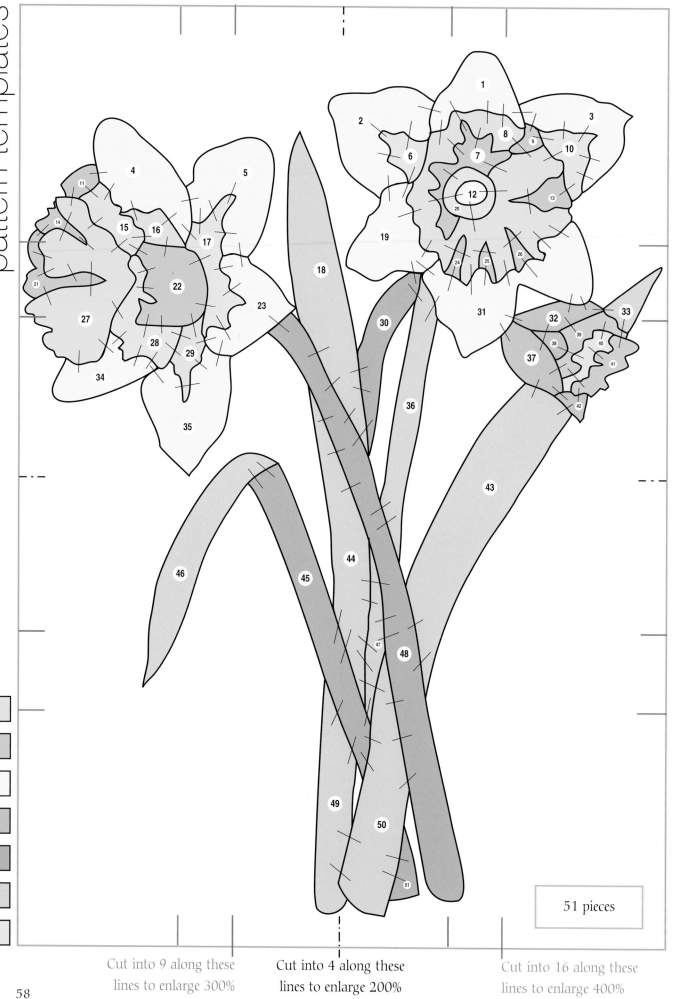

51 pieces

Cut into 9 along these
lines to enlarge 300%

Cut into 4 along these
lines to enlarge 200%

Cut into 16 along these
lines to enlarge 400%

Dutch Iris

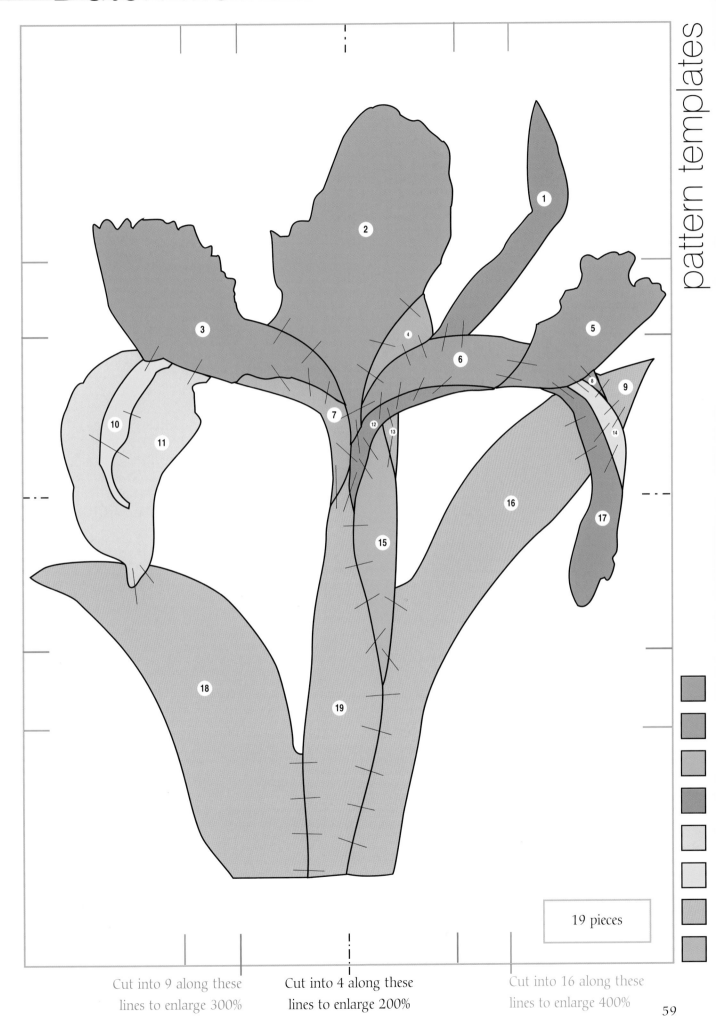

19 pieces

Cut into 9 along these
lines to enlarge 300%

Cut into 4 along these
lines to enlarge 200%

Cut into 16 along these
lines to enlarge 400%

59

Clematis

43 pieces

Cut into 9 along these
lines to enlarge 300%

Cut into 4 along these
lines to enlarge 200%

Cut into 16 along these
lines to enlarge 400%

Day lily

81 pieces

Cut into 9 along these
lines to enlarge 300%

Cut into 4 along these
lines to enlarge 200%

Cut into 16 along these
lines to enlarge 400%

Apple blossom

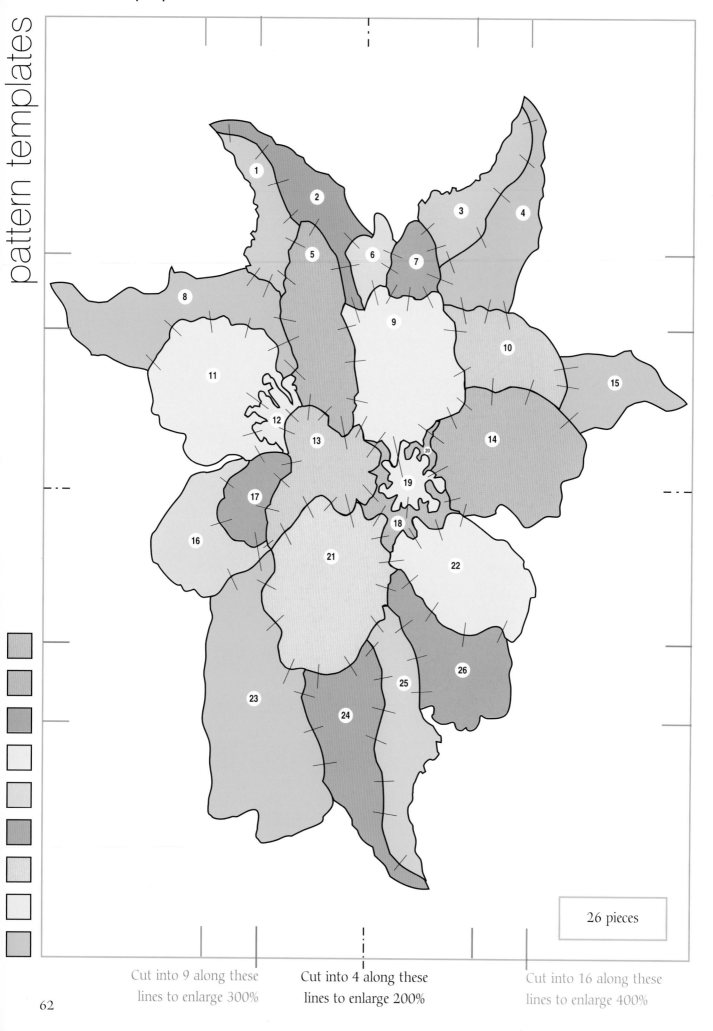

26 pieces

Cut into 9 along these
lines to enlarge 300%

Cut into 4 along these
lines to enlarge 200%

Cut into 16 along these
lines to enlarge 400%

White lily

118 pieces

Cut into 9 along these
lines to enlarge 300%

Cut into 4 along these
lines to enlarge 200%

Cut into 16 along these
lines to enlarge 400%

pattern templates

63 pieces

Cut into 9 along these
lines to enlarge 300%

Cut into 4 along these
lines to enlarge 200%

Cut into 16 along these
lines to enlarge 400%

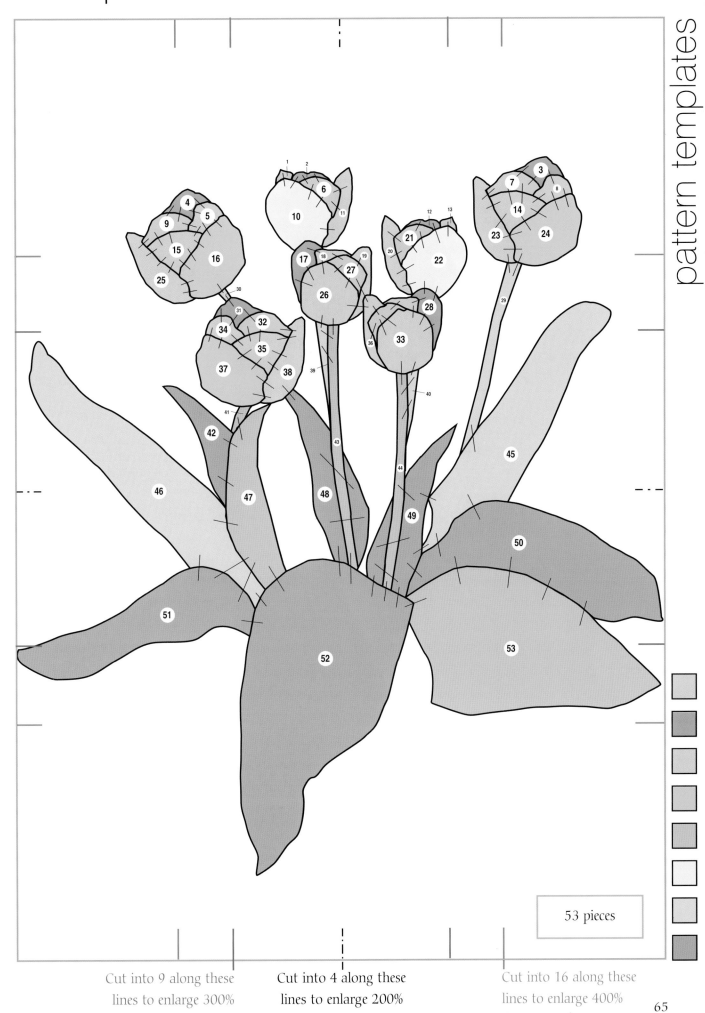

53 pieces

Cut into 9 along these
lines to enlarge 300%

Cut into 4 along these
lines to enlarge 200%

Cut into 16 along these
lines to enlarge 400%

pattern templates

28 pieces

14 pieces

42 pieces
Combined

Cut into 9 along these
lines to enlarge 300%

Cut into 4 along these
lines to enlarge 200%

Cut into 16 along these
lines to enlarge 400%

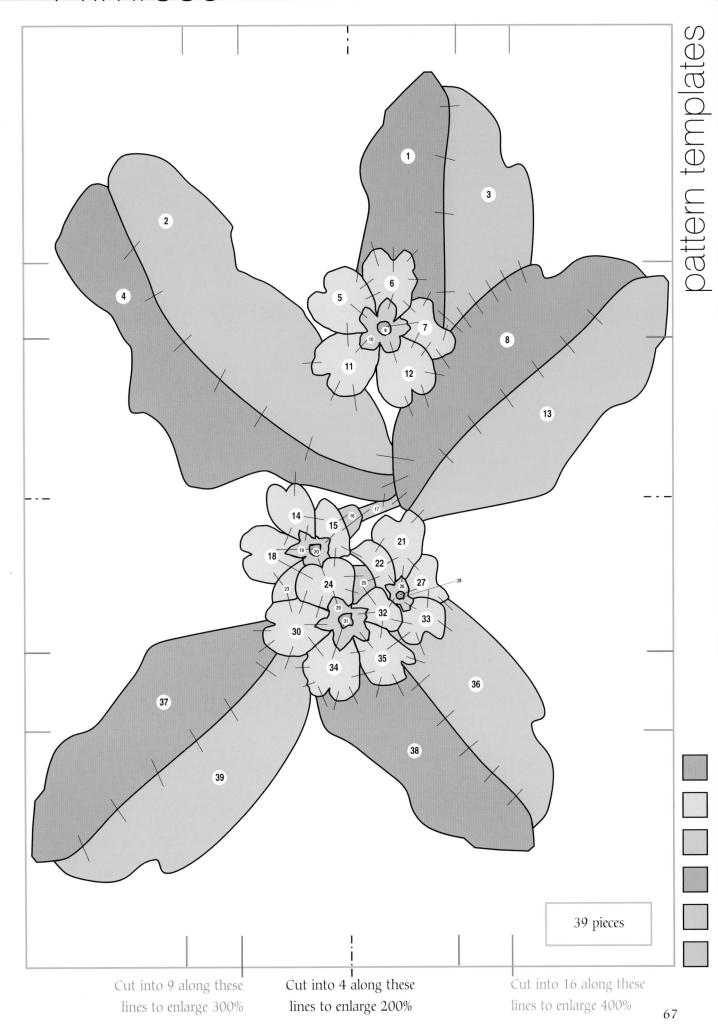

39 pieces

Cut into 9 along these
lines to enlarge 300%

Cut into 4 along these
lines to enlarge 200%

Cut into 16 along these
lines to enlarge 400%

141 pieces

Cut into 9 along these
lines to enlarge 300%

Cut into 4 along these
lines to enlarge 200%

Cut into 16 along these
lines to enlarge 400%

Poppy

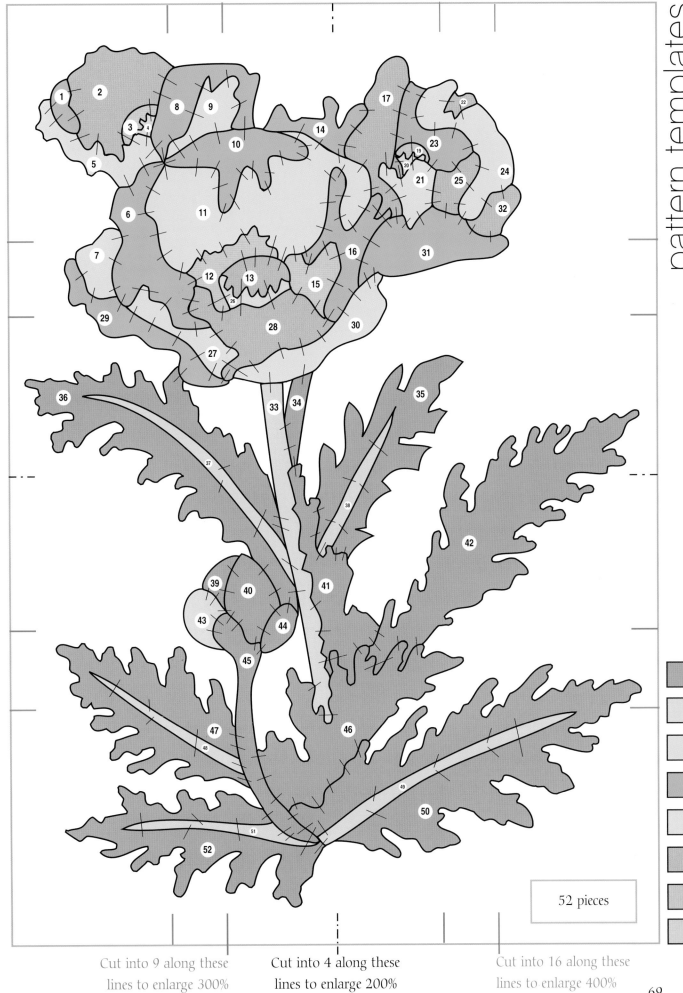

52 pieces

Cut into 9 along these
lines to enlarge 300%

Cut into 4 along these
lines to enlarge 200%

Cut into 16 along these
lines to enlarge 400%

pattern templates

64 pieces

Cut into 9 along these
lines to enlarge 300%

Cut into 4 along these
lines to enlarge 200%

Cut into 16 along these
lines to enlarge 400%

97 pieces

Cut into 9 along these
lines to enlarge 300%

Cut into 4 along these
lines to enlarge 200%

Cut into 16 along these
lines to enlarge 400%

71

62 pieces

Cut into 9 along these
lines to enlarge 300%

Cut into 4 along these
lines to enlarge 200%

Cut into 16 along these
lines to enlarge 400%

Completed projects
Angela's Gallery

Nasturtium

'This bud of love, by summer's ripening heat
May prove a beauteous flower
When next we meet.'
— William Shakespeare.

Gallery

Angela's Gallery

'A lily of a day
Is fairer far in May.
Although it fall and die that night
It was the plant and flower of light'
– Francis T Palgrove

'How bravely thou becom'st
thy bed fresh lily!
And whiter than the sheets.'
– William Shakespeare

Quilting can be used in the background to indicate different effects such as water, clouds or light rays.

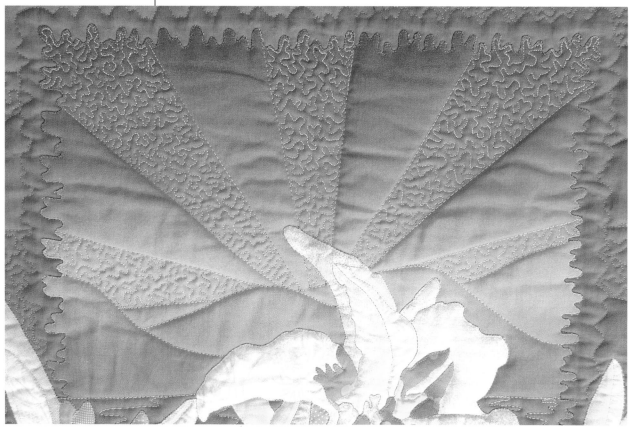

Day Lily

Dutch Iris

Apple Blossom

Beads and sequins hand stitched to the quilt can add texture and highlight areas of interest.

'Church-bells will chime, you will be mine, in apple blossom time.'
– Neville Fleeson

Angela's Gallery

Fuchsia

'I hate flowers .....
I paint them because they are cheaper
than models and they don't move!'
– Georgia O'Keefe.

White Lily

Completed projects
Angela's Gallery

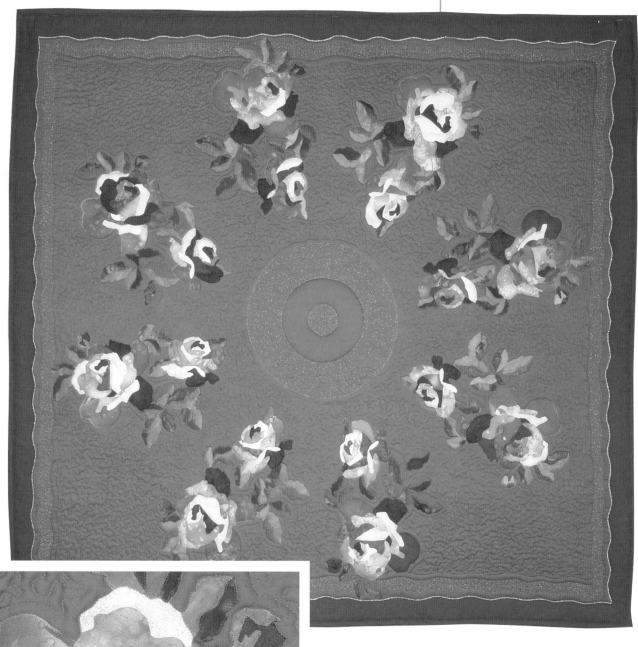

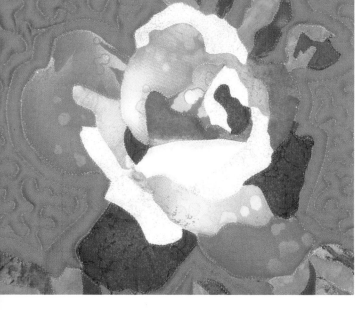

'Loveliest of lovely things are they
On earth that soonest pass away.
The rose that lives its little hour
Is prized beyond the sculptured flower.'
                    – William C. Bryant.

Roses

"There will I make thee a bed of roses,
With a thousand fragrant posies,
A cap of flowers, and a kirtle
Embroider'd all with leaves of myrtle."
- William Shakespeare

Completed projects

Angela's Gallery

Machine embroidery can be used to quilt, adding detail, texture and interest.

Poppies

The colour, quilting details and layout of a background can dramatically alter the setting of any flower.

Angela's Gallery

*'I am following Nature
without being able to grasp
her. I perhaps owe having
become a painter to flowers.'
– Claude Monet.*

Angela's Gallery

Iris and Primrose

Clematis

Completed projects
Angela's Gallery

Tulips

Contour quilting is a simple way to add textural interest to a background.

Using reversed flower patterns *(mirror image)* will increase the possibilities when planning grouped arrangements.

Completed projects
Angela's Gallery

A shaped edge requires binding to be cut at 45° on the bias.

Hibiscus

Red Poppy

'But pleasures are like poppies spread
You seize the flower, it's bloom is shed.
Or like the snow falls in the river
A moment white - then melts for ever.'
– Robert Burns

Gallery

Angela's Gallery

Daffodil

'I wander'd lonely as a cloud
That floats on high o'er vales and hills,
When all at once I saw a crowd,
A host, of golden daffodils;
Beside the lake, beneath the trees,
Fluttering and dancing in the breeze.'
– William Wordsworth

'And down the borders, well I know,
The poppy and the pansy blow...'
– Rupert Brooke

Pansy

Sew Easy Celtic

A really easy way to design original celtic knotwork patterns.

No artistic or mathematical skills are needed for great results. Based on drawing doodles, anyone can do it.

If you've ever cut out a paper snowflake this is for you.

Magic Celtic

More easy designing. This time using the 'Circle Slice Ruler' to draft accurate wedge shaped slices and more doodles to create 'pie slice' designs. They look amazingly complicated, but are really easy to draft and machine sew.

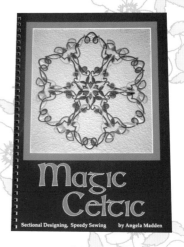

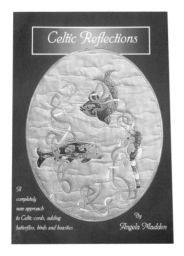

Celtic Reflections

A really different way to create celtic designs, created by using mirrors. Pieces of design are provided and the mirrors turn them into kaleidoscopic fun.

Infinite possibilities and all new sewing techniques too.

Appliqué and Roses

Two different appliqué techniques for blocks and borders. Vines and flowers are quick to make as the flowers are assembled by a unique multiple production system in which several 3D roses are made at the same time. Tudor, cabbage and dog roses are possible with 3D leaves to match.

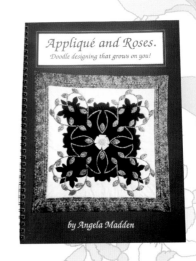

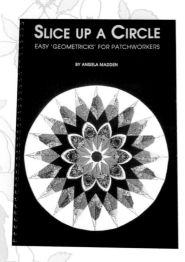

Slice up a Circle

Easy 'geometricks' with no maths. Compass, kaleidoscope and star designs fit together like a jigsaw. It is also easy to add curves without any tricky curved seam piecing.

Paradise Flowers

The ultimate book of floral geometric design. A unique and easy way to design and machine sew original flower patterns in traditional style, or as differently as you choose to make them.

Use the flowers singly, or be amazed at the effect of using them in multiples. Patterns can be used for patchwork, quilting, a new method of stained glass, stencilling, embroidery or trapunto. Design a flower and create a garden.

Pieceful Scenes

Give the traditional block of your choice a new look by linking them with a landscape in a 3D illusion. If you can draw a straight line using a pencil and a ruler, you can do this. Fast machine sewn assembly.

Photo Fabrications

Machine appliqué from family photos or other pictures. The easiest way ever to achieve true appliqué copies of landscapes, pets, houses, or people ... in fact whatever you wish. No 'art' involved just tracing and a little courage to have a go and find out how easy it can be when you know how!

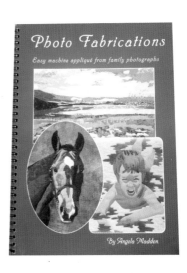

The Circle Slice Ruler

Takes all the inaccuracy out of drafting precise angles for pie slice designing. None of the problems with a protractor. Who cares how many degrees an angle contains ... you won't if you use this handy tool. Essential for using the books 'Magic Celtic', 'Slice up a Circle' and an optional extra to extend the possibilities of 'Paradise Flowers'.

The Multi-Plait tool

A unique tool which makes plaits easy to draw. Choose how wide they are and how many cords they contain. It even takes plaits around corners too. Great borders to accompany celtic designs.

The Feather Tool

Traditional feathered wreathes, borders, hearts, squares etc. are universally popular. This original tool will draw all of them, quickly and easily, in any size you would like to use.

Should you have difficulty obtaining any of these books they can be obtained mail order from ...

U.S.A.

Erica's Craft & Sewing Center
1320 N. Ironwood Dr.
South Bend, IN. 46615
(574) 233-3112

Country Stitches
2200 Coolidge
East Lansing, MI. 48823
(517) 351-2416

Quilting Books Unlimited
1309 Challenge Street
Batavia, IL. 60510
(630) 406-8374

Material Possessions
22600 C Lambert
Suite 905
Lake Forest, Ca. 92630
(949) 586-3418

Australia

Barossa Quilt & Craft Cottage,
P. O. Box 458.
Angaston. SA 5353
Tel: 088562 3212
www.barossaquilt.com.au

For current details of workshops and lectures

Please send a S.A.E. to the publication address at the start of this book or visit
Angela Madden's Website: **angelamadden.com**